# A Common Sense Approach to Discipline

## A Condensed Guide for Effective Discipline

By

Mike Stefanick

*A Book for Parents, Teachers and Counselors*

*A Book for Everyone*

AuthorHouse™
1663 Liberty Drive
Bloomington, IN 47403
www.authorhouse.com
Phone: 1 (800) 839-8640

Because of the dynamic nature of the Internet, any web addresses or links contained in this book may have changed
since publication and may no longer be valid. The views expressed in this work are solely those of the author and do not
necessarily reflect the views of the publisher, and the publisher hereby disclaims any responsibility for them.

Any people depicted in stock imagery provided by Getty Images are models,
and such images are being used for illustrative purposes only.
Certain stock imagery © Getty Images.

This book is printed on acid-free paper.

ISBN: 978-1-7283-2469-2 (sc)
ISBN: 978-1-7283-2470-8 (e)

Print information available on the last page.

Published by AuthorHouse 08/26/2019

authorHOUSE®

# Table of Contents

# Introduction

Are you a parent, teacher or counselor? Do you have a concern about discipline? Are you looking for a condensed guide for effective discipline? Then this book is for you. Even if you are a manager, administrator or leader this book could be for you too.

When you listen to the news or read the newspaper, you probably ask yourself what's going on with our kids. As a parent or grandparent have you ever said or heard someone say, "I don't know what to do with these kids? Or "I'm at my wits end with this child". As a teacher or counselor, have you ever said or heard someone say, "What's wrong with these kids today?" Recently we heard about the mother that had her children get out of her car and then drive off without them. She had to be at her wit's end and didn't know what else to do. What can we do? How can we keep these things from happening? If these are questions you have and you are looking for answers, then this book is for you.

It is felt that this guide is applicable for anyone but most specifically to parents, teachers, counselors, school administrators and/or anyone involved with or working with children. This book is a condensed and effective guide for discipline. This book can even be useful to managers, leaders and just about everyone.

Read this book and get Mike Stefanick's thoughts and insights into an effective guide for discipline. Mike will also include many of his thoughts and insights into preparing our children for the future and about life in general.

# The Author

Mike Stefanick is a retired Colonel and a retired Superintendent of Schools. Besides these, he has also served as a teacher, coach, assistant high school principal at 2 different secondary schools, a Director of Elementary Education, and a Mobil Therapist for disadvantaged youth. In the Army, Mike had numerous leadership and management positions. He has even managed a Census Bureau Office with approximately 600 employees. Mike has a vast amount of experience. He has worked with adults and children at all age levels and from all walks of life. Many of his positions required him to be primarily responsible for discipline. Among his educational accomplishments, he is a graduate of the Army's Command and General Staff College and has a Master's Degree in Counseling. He is also a recipient of the Konrad Lindenberg Memorial Award for his efforts in promoting parent involvement in schools and a recipient of the Leadership for Learning Award by the American Association of School Administrators for his effective style of educational leadership.

Mike is also a father, son, brother, and grand father. He is a 65 year old widower. He has 4 children and 4 grand children. Three of his children have a Master's Degree and the 4th has a Bachelor's Degree. Mike is very proud of all his children. In addition, all his children are in well respected professions and doing well.

# Discipline thoughts and insights....

Following are some of Mike's thoughts and insights, from his personal experiences and observations, about Discipline:

**Discipline is teaching** – Mike believes you train animals and you educate children.

**Expectations –** Expectations are the key ingredient to any effective discipline plan. Be you parent or teacher; tell your children what you want them to do and what you expect from them. Be positive. Children want to please you. Children will try to live up to your expectations. If you continually tell children they are bad or no good, don't be surprised if they grow up feeling and/or acting that way.

**No ultimatums** – Do not give children ultimatums unless you plan on keeping them. Ultimatums and threats do not motivate children. Ultimatums and threats build resentment and anger.

**Let your child know education is important –** If you let your child (ren) know education is important, they will grow up realizing that education is important; but, if you convey to your child (ren) that education is not important then they will grow up feeling that education is not important

**Children want to be disciplined** – Children want parameters. They will test you to see how far they can go. They want to know what they can and can not do. Sometimes their actions, like temper tantrums, are a vehicle used in determining their parameters.

**It is the surety of the discipline not the severity that makes the difference** – Make the consequences fit the infraction. A five minute timeout, if administered in the correct manner, in many cases will be just as effective as something more severe.

**Parents must be consistent and work as a team** – Don't send mixed signals to your children. Don't undermine each other. If you disagree on how to discipline a child, do it in private. And once you make a decision make it both of your decisions. Don't play good guy bad guy with your child or say it is the other parent's idea. Be a team. First and foremost you are their parent and not their friend. Not that you can not be their friend. But, do not shirk your responsibilities as a parent to be your child's friend. Your primary responsibility is to guide and support them

**Support the school and do not subscribe to the first story syndrome** – When your child tells you that something negative happened at school, get both sides before you fly off the handle and decide on exactly what you are to do. I have heard many parents say "my child doesn't lie to me" and I probably agree. They don't lie. Many times they just don't tell you the whole story. If your child comes home and says something wrong happened at school, refrain from jumping to conclusions or over reacting. Listen to your child's story without being judgmental. Then ask them something like "what do you think the school will say when I call them?" Don't be surprised if you get a second version before you call the school. Don't hesitate to call the school and get both sides. If there is a disagreement, you discuss it with school officials in private. Do not let your child know what buttons to push on you. If you have difficulty getting consistent stories try to arrange with school officials that when your child is involved in an incident that they call you at home or work and let the child tell you in their own words what happened while the school official is present. That way, misunderstandings can be resolved immediately.

**Don't ever say to your child – "I don't know what to do with you"** – Once you say that to your child, they say to themselves," If you don't know what to do with me then who does?" There is always something you can do. Sometime parents unknowingly will consistently blame the school and/or others for all the incidents their child is involved with and wrongly defend their child to the hilt. The child will ultimately recognize the rift between the school and the parents and begin to play games with both of you. Once a child senses that, especially if you are a parent that over reacts quickly, they will come home and tell you what they think you want to hear (whatever it is that pushes your button). You get angry at the school or school officials and over react. Then all of a sudden, after several situations like this, the child is in 8th or 9th grade and you, as a parent, are sitting with the counselor or principal saying," I don't know what to do with them", and by that time it may be too late. I am not implying that the school or school officials are always right. What I am saying is to learn to work with the school and school officials

**Discipline with dignity** – Do not belittle or degrade your child. This will only lead to a poor self esteem and bitterness by the child. Do not reward inappropriate behavior. Reward appropriate behavior. Try not to discipline out of anger. Because once something is said, you can apologize all you want but there is no way it can ever be taken back or forgotten.

**Discipline in private and praise in public** – As a parent or teacher try to always discipline in private and praise in public. As a teacher, and whenever possible, when you need to discipline a child, pull the child aside or take them out into the hall and discipline the child one on one. Do not try to embarrass or humiliate a child in front of other children or in front of their peers. When deserving and appropriate, do not forget to praise children in public.

**Do not over react** – Remain calm, do not over react. Make the punishment fit the offense. Be you parent or educator, do not give children ultimatums. And if you do make sure you follow through with them. Otherwise you will lose credibility. Concentrate on telling children what you want or expect them to do and not on what you don't expect them to do. Do not scream and holler or rant and rave; because, after a while all they hear is the noise and not the message. Many times children act up to get attention and when you over react in the classroom you play right into their hands. Some children feel negative attention is better than no attention at all.

**Stick to the issue** – When you are having a disciplinary session with a child, stick to the issue. Do not overwhelm the child with too many issues. Do not get side tracked, stick to the situation. Work on correcting one item at a time.

**Observe your children and/or students** – See who they are associating with. Notice the activities, interests and values of your children, students and those they pal around with.

**Let your children know you love them unconditionally.**

# Preparing Children for the Future

All good parents want their children to grow up and be productive citizens. They especially want them to be well rounded, good decision makers and successful. Good educators want to work with parents to do the same. At home the parent makes the difference. At school, the teacher makes the difference. When the home and the school work together, the chances that then child (ren) will be successful is increased significantly.

Following are some of Mike's thoughts and insights from his observations and personal experience on how to prepare our children for the future:

**Independent vs dependent** – Teach children to be independent not dependent. Do not talk for your child when they are asked a question and they are capable of answering for themselves. Do not do everything for your child.

**Prepare children for their world** – Make sure you are preparing children for their world and not yours. Their world will be different than yours or ours. As a matter of fact, I can almost guarantee you 100%, that most of the jobs that our present 2nd and 3rd graders will do have not been invented yet.

**Get your child(ren) an education** – I am talking about an education or marketable training beyond high school. "I truly feel and believe that with an education your child(ren) will have a **chance** to do what they want in life; but, without an education they will do what society dictates".

**Skills to teach your children** – There are two (2) main skills I would encourage all parents and all educators to instill in their children. Those two skills are: (1) people skills and (2) problem solving skills. These 2 skills coupled with technical competence will guarantee children success.

**Want versus a need** – Teach your children early in life the difference between what they want and what they need. Many children grow up believing that what they want is more important than what they need and ultimately leads many of them to financial disaster.

# Tips to Live By

Following are some of Mike's thoughts and insights from his personal experiences and observations about life in general:

**To be successful at life –** Put family first. If you put your family first, it does make many decisions much easier.

**To be successful at work** – Make your boss look good. When you are praised or given credit include them as part of your response. Unless it is unsafe or unethical, you may have to accept the blame for some mistakes.

**Motivate by trust** – There are mainly two ways of motivating people. One is by fear and the other is by trust. Motivating by fear stymies creativity and innovation, reduces risk taking, and produces only what is expected. People usually work in an environment like this because they have to work there. Motivating by trust encourages creativity, innovation, risk taking and thinking out of the box. It also leads to a more open environment. People usually work in an environment like this because they enjoy working there.

**Attitude is everything –** Be positive. See the good in people. Try to find the good in everything.

**Count your blessings –** First thing every morning, count your blessings. Appreciate what you have.

**In everybody's life a little rain must fall –** No matter how hard we try, sometimes things just go wrong. The important thing is how you deal with it or react to it. Remember, once something happens, you can not change it. Learn from your mistakes and find a way to go forward. Many times the best advice is FIDO (forget it and drive on).

**Blessing in disguise** – Sometimes good things happen in life when you least expect it. Sometimes in life, something may have seemed devastating at the time but when you look back you realize it was a blessing in disguise.

**Feeling down –** Whenever you feel down, do something nice for someone without expecting anything in return. Have a sense of humor. Do not take yourself too seriously.

**Every problem has a solution –** We may not like it, but every problem has a solution. Sometimes, doing nothing is a solution. Problems should be seen as challenges. Think WIN–WIN.

**More than one way to do everything** – Many times, you will hear Mike say the following when dealing with issues, "there are many ways to get to

Pittsburgh, and because you don't go the way I go doesn't mean you won't get there".

**If you always do what you always did, you'll always get what you always got**

**If you keep doing the same thing over and over again expecting different results –** Einstein called that insanity. Mike agrees with that.

**Do the right things** - There is no right way to do the wrong thing.

**Be wary of those that try to bring you down to their level**

**Always have a plan B** – Many times in life things do not work out as they are planned. Be it work, careers, decisions, driving a car or whatever, always anticipate other what if possibilities.

**Passion** – Know what you are passionate about. Know what your passions are. Also know what buttons people can push to set you off. Everybody has them.

**Time** - Time has a way of healing.

**Be patient –** Timing is very important

**Always have something to do tomorrow –** In the meantime, don't forget to have fun and enjoy life.

**Decisions** - Every decision you make is the right one, only time will tell if it is a good one or a bad one. Remember whenever you make a decision; you are actually deciding who you are going to tick off. When making a decision, always think WIN-WIN.

**Relationships** - If you don't like the way your relationship is going with someone, then change the way you deal with that person. Don't expect the other person to change. They will only change when they are ready and when they want to.

**Leader vs manager** – There is a difference. A leader has the vision, the passion and a plan to reach that vision. A leader sets the long term goals and short term goals. A leader provides the guidance and parameters to accomplish the mission. A leader monitors and adjusts as necessary. A manager puts the right people, in the right place at the right time to get the job done. A manager is the doer.

**If you think you can or if you think you can't, you're right**

**Advice** - When given advice, take some and leave some

# A Challenge to All Educators

I want to use this page to make a personal challenge to all educators. Good educators are a very caring, compassionate and concerned group of people. They have a keen sense for knowing and determining when some children are headed down the wrong path even before they do. So, at the beginning of each school year, I challenge all educators to establish the following as a personal goal:

**One of my personal goals for this school year is to turn at least one child or student around.**

Left to Right:

Kevin – Master's Degree in Engineering Management – Penn State University

Michelle – Master's Degree in Strategic Planning – also a CPA

Ruthann – Bachelor's Degree – Hotel and Hospitality Management – Indiana University of Pennsylvania

Kara – Master's Degree in Psychology – Liberty University

Mike – Retired – Master's Degree and BS Degree from Indiana University of Pennsylvania, Administrative Certifications from Penn State University, attended University of South Carolina Graduate School

Printed in the United States
By Bookmasters